PORN
IN THE
PEW

Austin Brothers Publishing
www.austinbrotherspublishing.com

PRAISE FOR PORN IN THE PEW

This book is packed with facts and helpful information. "There's Still Hope" is a ministry that will walk with you hand in hand to see God's victory. Mark and Beth have experienced God's grace and restoration in their own lives. I more than endorse them. I salute them for being obedient, transparent servants willing to help others experience Christ-centered recovery.

Dr. Jay Gross
Senior Pastor, West Conroe Baptist Church
Conroe, Texas

Mark Denison has been my dear friend for over 35 years. He is spiritually in tune and culturally relevant. His most recent book, Porn in the Pew, is a must read, combining years of scholarship blended with his own story to create a life-giving book for those who struggle with addiction and a tool for church leaders who seek to be restorative, healing communities of grace.

Ray Waters
Senior Pastor, Village Church
Atlanta, Georgia

Mark has drawn from his own experience as a pastor and a recovering person to write a great guide to help the church navigate some very choppy waters. This is the kind of practical and biblical advice we need.

Greg Oliver
Founder, Awaken Ministry for Sex/Porn Addiction
Birmingham, Alabama

Porn in the Pew is both enlightening and from the heart. It provides desperately needed insight for how to minister and respond to those in the pew as well as the pulpit, who are impacted by the epidemic of sex and porn addiction. I applaud Dr. Denison for his work. I highly recommend it!

Jason Smith
Senior Pastor, Good Life Church
Bradenton, Florida

Mark Denison fell into a hole. Rather than wallow there, he had the courage to climb out. Now he's helping other men find their way to freedom. If you want to be free, read Porn in the Pew. It's a great resource for those who struggle with porn or sex addiction, as well as for church leaders who wish to confront this massive problem.

David Murrow
Author, Why Men Hate Going to Church

Pornography is a silent crisis within the church. Everyone knows it is a problem, but few are speaking up with constructive solutions. Mark sweeps away taboos and tackles the topic with honesty and clarity, providing real-world solutions for the church.

Steve Bezner
Senior Pastor, Houston's Northwest Baptist Church
Houston, Texas

Faith, hope, and love . . . I'm so glad that HOPE is surrounded by our faith and God's love. Thank you, Mark and Beth, for all three! Like the old song says, "It is no secret what God can do. What he's done for others, he can do for you." Porn in the Pew is a great resource for churches and church leaders. I highly recommend it!

Dr. Dennis Swanberg
Author, No More Secrets

Mark points out two great truths. Those addicted to porn are on the road to destruction, and Christ has a higher purpose. God has raised this ministry to help you on your journey toward recovery. Every church leader needs to read Porn in the Pew.

Ken Sigler
Senior Pastor, Grace Baptist Church
St. Louis, Missouri

Pornography is everywhere. It is stealing the lives of our men, women, and children. We must help those trapped in a life of porn and sex addiction. That's what Mark Denison is doing with Porn in the Pew. He's done his homework. He has laid out a plan to bring freedom to the church and her leaders.

Tim Boyd
Senior Pastor, Westside Christian Church
Bradenton, Florida

Porn in the Pew is for pastors and churches who seek to help those caught in the snare of pornography and sexual addiction. Having known Mark for 40 years, I know the brokenness and healing he and Beth have experienced. Mark has combined his personal experience with biblical principles to help others be set free.

Phil Herrington
Senior Pastor, First Baptist Church
Coldspring, Texas

Porn in the Pew

Confronting the Issue Nobody
Wants to Talk About

Mark Denison D.Min.

Porn in the Pew

Confronting the Issue Nobody wants to Talk About

Mark Denison D.Min.

Published by Austin Brothers Publishing,

Fort Worth, Texas

www.abpbooks.com

ISBN978-1-7324846-3-4

Printed in the United States of America

2018 -- First Edition

I humbly dedicate this book to those whom God has used to lead me into a lifelong journey of recovery, beginning with Beth, my wife and best friend since 1983. I am grateful for those who have walked this road with me. I dedicate this work to pastors and faithful believers who continue to battle the demons of porn and sexual addiction. Finally, I am grateful to each of the three churches I was blessed to pastor over thirty-one wonderful years.

Contents

Contents

FOREWORD

It's the thing nobody in the church is talking about. It kills more marriages, drains more hearts, and ends more ministries than anything else. Still, nobody talks about it. We pretend it isn't there or that it will somehow go away—if we only ignore it long enough.

It's the elephant in the church. Pornography. Sex addiction.

We know that most of the men in church on Sunday are viewing porn at home on Monday. Or at work. Or on their phones.

The news for pastors isn't much better. One survey revealed that 37 percent of pastors battle porn. Most of them have given in and given up.

Still, nobody is talking about it—until now.

That's what this book is all about. We are going to talk about it. It won't be easy, but we're going to do it anyway. We are going to ask the tough questions and provide real answers. Nothing will be off limits.

If you suffer from porn or sex addiction, we will give you the tools necessary for a lifetime of recovery. If you are tired of the inner war between loving God and feeding your impulses, we offer hope. If you are a church leader wondering how to deal with porn in the pew—or in the pulpit—we provide practical steps to follow.

If you are a pastor, sincerely loving and serving God while battling demons nobody else sees, we have hope for you as well.

This is not for the faint of heart. It is for those who want to be well, and who want healthy churches and healthy pastors. It is for those willing to confront the issue nobody is talking about. It's time to talk about it—***Porn in the Pew***.

INTRODUCTION

What once was relegated to massage parlors and adult bookstores has infiltrated the church. What used to be the sin of the most depraved is bringing down the most godly—some from the highest pedestals of the church. The depravity that once filled pastors' sermons is now attacking their hearts. What the church has openly condemned for decades, she now secretly embraces.

The child growing up in the 1960s and 70s first saw porn in his dad's closet—if at all. The child of the 80s and 90s saw it in the convenience store, not as well disguised as it once was. The boy (or girl) of today first sees porn on a computer or mobile device by age 11. And one's church identity and spiritual persuasion have almost no correlation to his or her porn habits. It transcends all churches and denominations.

Is porn really that big of a problem for those who follow Christ? The evidence is in, and the answer is a resounding "YES!" While 64 percent of American men view porn monthly, among the men in evangelical churches, the number is 62 percent— nearly the same. In some segments of the population, porn use is actually higher among believers than nonbelievers. Clearly, we have a problem.

On Sunday morning, Joe Christian goes to church where he bows to the God of heaven. And on Sunday evening, Joe Christian goes to his secret place where he bows to the god of porn—more often on Sunday than any other day of the week. Church, it's clear; we have a problem.

At a time when 95 percent of Christian men have viewed porn, we have a problem. At a time when 54 percent of pastors view porn, we are at a crossroads. At a time when 64 percent of student pastors have struggled with porn, we need answers.

Yes, church, we have a problem. Church—you have a problem. Every church in America has the same problem. Porn and sex addiction are ripping apart more marriages and destroying more lives than anything else. It has become the enemy's primary tool.

Church, how will you respond? You have only three options.

- Ignore it.
- Condemn it.
- Address it.

Again, this book is not for the faint of heart. Nor is it for First Delusional Church—where they think the problem is down the street. Nor is this written for those who embrace condemnation over redemption, judgment over grace, despair over hope.

Church, we have a real problem that demands real answers. To that end, we will address five questions:

1. How bad is the problem?
2. Can you love God and porn at the same time?
3. What are the steps to recovery?
4. How can the church respond effectively?
5. What about porn in the pulpit?

MY STORY

I am a sex addict.

I can't really say where it started, but after hundreds of hours in therapy, it is apparent that isolation as a young child started me on my path. It usually does. But mine was a mostly happy childhood, apart from isolated instances of abuse (sexual and otherwise—none family related).

We didn't go to church much, but when a local bus ministry invaded our apartments, my brother and I became frequent riders to a nearby church with an active student ministry. Within a few months, we both came to faith in Christ. It wasn't long after that that we followed God's call to ministry. We were baptized the same day and licensed to the ministry the same day.

I went to an incredible Christian University where I was blessed to meet professors whose lives continue to impact me forty years later. My education continued with an M.Div. and D.Min. from a large Baptist Seminary. While working on my master's degree, Beth and I planted a church in the Houston area. We stayed there for nearly eighteen years. Then we followed God's call to another church in north Texas in 2001 and later back to a wonderful church near Houston in 2010.

My ministry was strong. I was blessed to work with great staffs and church leaders. Along the way, I served as chair of the board of trustees at my alma mater—three times. I wrote Sunday school material for my Baptist state convention. I served as a chaplain for the *Houston Rockets* for five seasons. I wrote a 365-day devotional book. Life was good—except for one thing.

I was—and am—a sex addict.

Beth had known I had a problem, but she didn't know how serious it was. In 2013 I entered recovery. That included a full three-day clinical disclosure with a polygraph test. It meant getting into 12-step meetings and extensive therapy with a CSAT (certified sex addiction therapist). It meant getting honest—totally honest—for the first time in my life.

In 2014 my past was discovered and exposed to a few men in my church. We met, and they graciously accepted my resignation without sharing any of the details with the congregation. I simply resigned "for personal reasons."

Now I had two choices. I could pop up someplace where they don't do great background checks and serve another church. I almost did that, but I turned down the chance to serve a megachurch in another part of the country.

My second option was to enter the private workforce. And I almost did that as well, but I turned down a generous offer to work for a company owned by a dear friend.

Both options were attractive, but God had other plans. He had a third option, one we would have never imagined.

God wanted Beth and me to make our problem our platform. So we began the work of preparation for ministry—all over again. For me, that meant going back to school. I earned a master's degree in addiction recovery from *Liberty University* and was accepted into the *American Association of Christian Counselors* (AACC). For Beth, that meant becoming a certified life coach and a certified partner recovery coach by the *American Association of Sex Addiction Therapists* (AASAT).

And then, five years into my recovery, we were ready. God has led us to bring hope to those who suffer. We serve addicts, spouses, churches, and pastors. We offer one-on-one coaching as well as group work. We speak to church groups. I work with pastors in several states. I design a customized 90-Day Recovery Plan and work with men from as far away as India and Ireland.

But while ministering to others, my own journey continues. I continue to attend two *Sexaholics Anonymous* (SA) meetings every week. I have a sponsor—an amazing man to whom I am indebted beyond words. And I sponsor about ten men in the program. I read recovery material every morning, starting with the *Life Recovery Bible* (which our ministry gives to everyone who asks).

I tell the men I work with that my greatest asset in helping them is not my degree in addiction recovery, the years of sobriety and recovery that I have achieved in my personal life, or the materials I have written.

What I have to offer more than anything else is that I am sober today.

In 1975 I responded to God's call to pastoral ministry. In 2014 that ministry died. But the best was yet to come. A dear friend, days after I resigned from my last church, assured me that the second half of my ministry would be my most impactful. (I hope he's right—that would mean I will live to be 100!)

I still believe in the church. When we moved to Florida from Texas, we joined a local church. My pastor has known my story since the year we joined his church. I pick up the donuts each Sunday. I am the head greeter. I serve on the prayer team and the finance team. I help with small groups and assimilation. I told my pastor—who has received me with incredible grace—that whatever he asks of me, the answer will be "Yes."

So we minister as wounded warriors to the body of Christ. We believe the only hope for real sobriety and lasting recovery is found in the Higher Power who is Jesus Christ. We are honored to serve him in ways we never imagined before.

This ministry is for the church, pastors, and church leaders. It is time to talk about what nobody is talking about—the elephant in the church. Porn. Sex addiction. The masks must come off. The veil must be lifted.

It is time for the church of today to be the church of yesterday—the one the Bible talks about. "Confess your faults one to another, that you may be healed" (James 5:16). If we can be part of that movement, it will all be worth it. But if we can help just one man, one woman, one pastor, or one church—it will still be worth it.

I am a Christ follower, husband, and dad. And I am a sex addict. Not just any sex addict—a recovering sex addict—one who welcomes you to join me on the road to recovery. The journey continues . . .

How Bad Is the Problem?

We know there is a problem. If you didn't know that, you wouldn't be reading this right now. The real question is, how bad is the problem?

Dr. Jimmy Draper, retired president of LifeWay, says, "It appears the sin of choice among Christians today is pornography."[1] A recent *Barna* study reveals that 93 percent of pastors see porn as a rising problem in the church, yet only seven percent of all churches have a plan of response.

Dozens of recent studies confirm the magnitude of the porn problem in America and the

---

1   Joe Dallas, The Game Plan: The Men's 30-Day Strategy for Attaining Sexual Purity. (Nashville, TN: Thomas Nelson Publishing, 2005), 4.

church. Here we will consider data provided by *Focus on the Family, The Barna Group, Josh McDowell, Christianity Today, The London School of Economics, Covenant Eyes, Pastors.com, OneNewsNow.com, Proven Men Ministries, Expastors.com, CBS News, Zogby Poll, HuffPost, WebRoot, NBC News, CBN,* and others.

THE GENERAL PORN PROBLEM

Let's consider a sampling of recent data. This is not meant to serve as a comprehensive study, nor do we claim absolute accuracy.

- Porn is a $12 billion industry in the United States. (*NBC News*)
- The top porn site had 23 billion visits in 2016. (*Covenant Eyes*)
- Twenty-five percent of all search engine searches are porn related. (*healthymind.com*)
- Porn sites get more visits than *Netflix, Amazon,* and *Twitter* combined. (*HuffPost*)
- Child porn is a $3 billion industry in the United States. (*TopTenReviews*)
- Forty million Americans view porn regularly. (*CBN*)

- On average, the first view of porn occurs at age 11. (*internet-filter-review.com*)
- Ninety percent of children ages 8–16 have viewed porn on the internet. (*London School of Economics*)
- Seventy-one percent of porn use is online. (*Barna*)
- Thirty-five percent of all internet downloads are porn related. (*WebRoot*)
- The most watched porn site was viewed for 4.6 billion hours last year. (*Covenant Eyes*)
- There are 4.2 million porn websites. (*archkck.org*)
- Hotel viewership for adult films is 55 percent. (*cbsnews.com*)
- Between 10 percent and 18 percent of men admit to sexual addiction. (*internet-filterreview.com, ChurchMilitant.com*)
- While the U.S. makes up 4.3 percent of the world's population, it represents 12.4 percent of porn use, three times the world's average use of porn. (*NBC News*)
- Porn increases marital infidelity by 300 percent. (*WebRoot*)

THE PORN EPIDEMIC IN THE CHURCH

Is porn use by Christians less widespread than among non-believers? Yes, but not by much. Clearly, porn is the greatest unaddressed threat to the stability and credibility of the Church. Here is the data.

- Sixty-two percent of evangelical men view porn monthly, compared to 64 percent of non-believers. (*Proven Men Ministries*)
- Ninety-five percent of Christian men have viewed porn. (*Barna*)
- Seventy-eight percent of Christian men view porn several times a year. (*Josh McDowell*)
- Fifty-three percent of men who attended *Promise Keeper* meetings viewed porn the next week. (*Pastors.com*)
- Thirteen percent of Christian men say they are addicted to porn; another five percent say they might be. (*Proven Men Ministries*)
- Christian men view porn at work at the same level as non-Christian men. (*ChurchMilitant.com*)
- Forty-seven percent of Christian families say porn is a problem in their home. (*Focus on the Family*)

- The most popular day for Christians to view porn is Sunday. (*Expastors.com*)
- Seven percent of Christians view porn several times a day. (*ChurchMilitant.com*)
- More Christians view porn daily than non-Christians. (*ChurchMilitant.com*)
- Over 50 percent of church staffs struggle with cybersex. (*Covenant Eyes*)
- Twenty-nine percent of born-again adults feel porn is morally acceptable. (*Barna*)
- Fifty-seven percent of pastors say porn addiction is the most damaging issue in their congregation. (*Christians and Sex Leadership Journal* Survey)

PORN AMONG CLERGY

Attaining reliable data on porn use among clergy is not easy. It is assumed that pastors underreport their porn use. We will address this more in the final section of this book, "Porn in the Pulpit."

- Fifty-four percent of pastors have viewed porn in the last year. (*Pastors.com*)
- Thirty-seven percent of pastors admit to a struggle with porn. (*Christianity Today*)

- Thirty percent of pastors have viewed porn in the last month. (*Pastors.com*)
- Twenty-five percent of pastors have purchased printed porn. (*Barna*)
- Twenty-one percent of student pastors and 14 percent of senior pastors struggle with porn "right now." (*Barna*)
- Twelve percent of student pastors and five percent of senior pastors say they are addicted to porn. (*Barna*)
- Among pastors who call the Focus on the Family toll-free helpline, 70 percent say they are addicted to porn. (*Focus on the Family*)
- Only 25 percent of pastors have any form of accountability. (*Patrick Means*)

PORN USE AMONG SUB-GROUPS

The fastest growth area of porn use is among women. And as we have seen, the porn audience is steadily getting younger, with the first porn view coming by the age of 11. But other alarming data shows porn and sex addiction impact specific sub-groups more than others.

First, consider the data among men:
- Seventy-two percent of all men view porn sites. (*archkck.org*)
- Fifty percent of men struggle with porn. (*Covenant Eyes*)
- Twenty-five percent of men hide their internet browser. (*Barna*)
- Seventy-nine percent of men ages 18–30 view porn. (*Barna*)
- Sixty-seven percent of men ages 31–49 view porn. (*Barna*)
- Forty-nine percent of men ages 50–68 view porn. (*Barna*)
- Thirty-three percent of millennials say they might be addicted to sex. (*Barna*)
- Porn use among women is on the rise.
- Twenty-eight percent of those admitting to sex addiction are women. (*internet-filter-review.com*)
- Thirty-four percent of readers of *Today's Christian Women* use internet porn.
- Twenty percent of women in church struggle with porn. (*Covenant Eyes*)
- Seventy percent of women view porn regularly. (*Zogby*)

- Thirty-three percent of women ages 18–24 view porn regularly. *(Josh McDowell*)
- Thirteen percent of women have accessed porn at work. (*archkck.org*)
- Six percent of all Christian women seek porn at least once a month. (*Barna*)
- Women are more likely to view "hardcore" porn than men. (*Covenant Eyes*)
- Eighteen percent of Christian women view porn "a few times a year," compared to just 15 percent of non-Christian women. (*ChurchMilitant.com*)
- Sixty percent of women have significant struggles with lust. (*ChristianNet Poll*)

A BRIEF SUMMARY

Putting all the numbers together, we find some clear trends in the porn epidemic of today. Here, we will highlight a few of those trends and offer summary data.

- Christians view porn almost as often as non-Christians.
- Men view porn more than women, but among women, porn use is proliferating.

- Younger adults view porn more than older adults.
- The number of sex addicts is 10–18 percent of the population.
- At least 50 percent and as high as 78 percent of Christians view porn.
- Porn use is an alarming problem among pastors, especially student pastors, and clergy generally have no accountability.

CAN YOU LOVE GOD AND PORN AT THE SAME TIME?

This is a question many of us have wrestled with mightily. In the manmade hierarchy of sin, porn and sexually addictive activities rank near the top, somewhere above lying, profanity, and substance abuse, and only slightly beneath the unpardonable sin. For the pastor, it is deemed far worse to view porn one day than to not have a personal devotion time for a year. We define a person by what they do more than by who they are.

Of course, none of this justifies a single instance of porn use or illegitimate sexual acting out. But that's not the question. Most would agree the sex addict can love God—apart from his addiction. But can he love God while still in his addiction? The way we answer that as a church means everything.

It will determine how we respond to the epidemic of porn in the pew.

While the limitations of this book do not allow for an exhaustive response to the question, we will briefly address it head-on. Can you love God and porn at the same time? I propose six responses that will answer that question.

A PRACTICAL RESPONSE

Let's answer the question with a series of smaller questions. Can a person eat too much chocolate and still love God? Can he play too much golf and still love God? Can a man say something inappropriate and still love God? Did David love God and Bathsheba at the same time? Did Peter love the Lord he denied?

John the Divine made it clear in his first epistle that a man who says he has moved beyond sin is not telling the truth. So whether he mismanages his diet, time, money, speech, or sex drive—all forbidden in Scripture—he is still the same sinner saved by grace. Nelson Mandela said it well. "I am not a saint unless you think of a saint as a sinner who keeps on trying."

Whether a man can view porn without shame is a different topic. Can a man indulge in sexual promiscuity void of shame or conviction, without repentance, while at the same moment embracing an intimate spiritual connection? I think not. But can he still be in the fight of his life, a fight for purity not yet won, and love God? I say yes. In fact, I suggest that if that were not true, that man would have no hope.

A HISTORICAL RESPONSE

The Apostle Paul wrote, "I do not the good I want to do, but the evil I do not want to do—this I keep on doing" (Romans 7:19). So how is it that the great apostle, clearly in love with God, had an ongoing struggle with sin? Is this a blight on his character? Was he not a man of integrity? How can it be possible that a man sincerely loves and serves God while struggling with ongoing sin? J.I. Packer offers brilliant insight: "Paul wasn't struggling with sin because he was such a sinner. Paul was struggling with sin because he was such a saint."[2] We'll unpack that later.

---

2   Kenneth Berding, A Key Insight about Romans 7 from a Conversation with J.I. Packer. (La Mirada, CA: Biola

Clearly, history is full of examples of men in love with God who simultaneously struggled—with sin, temptation, doubt, and depression.

Consider a few biblical examples. Job questioned God's plan for his life when he asked, "Why didn't I perish at birth?" (Job 3:11). David, the adulterer, was a man after God's own heart (Acts 13:22). In the midst of his struggles with sin he confessed, "My guilt has overwhelmed me like a burden too heavy to bear" (Psalm 38:4). Elijah said, "I have had enough, Lord. Take my life" (1 Kings 19:4). Those are hardly the words of a preacher who had it all together. Moses killed a man (Exodus 2), Jonah despised the conversions of thousands of sinners and wanted to die (Jonah 4), Jeremiah cursed the day he was born (Jeremiah 20:14), and Peter denied even knowing Jesus—three times (Luke 22).

The hall of fame of great Christian leaders is filled with men and women who struggled. Luther doubted his own salvation; Spurgeon battled fits of feeling worthless; Calvin battled unbelief; C. S. Lewis endured long periods of personal doubt; Mother Teresa spoke of her personal hypocrisy and doubts about her faith, and Pope Francis has confessed to struggles with doubt.

University, April 4, 2012).

When asked by David Frost to describe his life with one word, Billy Graham said, "Failure."[3]

Let's return to our question. Can a man love God and porn at the same time? Unless one sets porn aside from the thousands of other struggles that godly men have battled in the midst of their spiritual walks, the historic response must be "Yes." If Peter can deny knowing Jesus weeks before the Pentecost sermon; if Elijah can run from God on the immediate heels of his greatest triumph; if David can commit adultery and have a man put to death while still leading Israel to her greatest heights; if Luther, Calvin, and Mother Teresa could struggle with their faith while impacting the world with the imprint of Christ—yes, a person can love God and porn at the same time.

But let's be clear. The man who battles porn addiction while seeking a dynamic walk with God will be the model of the "double-minded man" of James 1:8. If you love God and are still mired in your addiction, prepare for countless sleepless nights, unfulfilled relationships, long periods of guilt and shame, powerlessness, and unspeakable despair and depression.

---

3   David Frost, Prime Time Live TV Special. (PBS, February 3, 1993).

The good news for the sex addict is that while he may still love porn that doesn't mean he has to be enslaved by it. I love chocolate-filled *Shipley's* donuts. There was a time when I ate at least one every day. To this day, when I drive by a *Shipley's*, I am triggered. I remember the taste as distinctly as if I had indulged minutes before. I want another donut, for the last one only satisfied for the moment. But I know eating another donut will only harm my body, in disobedience to the command about being the temple of the Holy Spirit (1 Corinthians 6:19). But knowing the Scripture doesn't remove the craving. My 267 days of donut sobriety has yet to remove my love for chocolate-filled donuts. So yes, I love those donuts at the same time I love God.

If you are addicted to porn, your love for God will likely not take that away. The honest question is not which one you will love, but rather which one will you serve.

AN EXPERIENTIAL RESPONSE

I hesitate to offer an experiential response to the big question—Can a man love God and porn at the same time? My theology informs me that personal experience is trumped by biblical revelation. So don't read too much into personal experience.

I can only speak for myself. While living in my addiction, the cycle introduced by sex addiction trailblazer Patrick Carnes described my experience perfectly. The four phases of the addiction cycle are preoccupation, ritualization, compulsive sexual behavior, and despair. For the believer, that final phase—despair—is usually filled with genuine repentance and brokenness. Again, I can only speak for myself. While living in my addiction, I read the Bible nearly every day. I maintained an active prayer list. I practiced the spiritual disciplines on a daily basis. I shared my faith with others. I was in men's groups, Bible studies, and at least three worship services per week.

In response to my addiction, I sought counseling. I was sincere about seeking help, as I spent thousands of dollars on therapy. I went to Stephen Arterburn's men's retreat. I fasted for six days, begging God to remove my destructive desires. I confessed my sin, repented of my sin, and prayed some more. I shared my struggles with my men's accountability partners, read countless books on sex addiction, and I prayed some more. I confessed

my struggles—not all of them, but some of them—
to my wife and my best friend, and I prayed some
more. I confessed my struggles to God when alone
with him on the mountain, by the lake, and on the
beach. Then I prayed some more.

Still, I was addicted. I didn't want to be, but I
was.

As of this writing, I have attended over five
hundred 12-step meetings. I try to get to two each
week, to this day. I have never been in a fellowship
that is more real, genuine, and transparent than
a good 12-step meeting. Men share their greatest
struggles. They share things they have never told
another human being. So, as much as is possible, in
those meetings we really get to know each other. I
mean really know each other.

And this is what I have learned. My groups are
filled with God-loving, Christ-following, Bible-read-
ing, church-attending men. By a disproportionate
number, I have found Christians in 12-step meetings. They are some of the most genuine, spiritual
men in my life. We text Bible verses back and forth
throughout the week. We pray for one another. We
share our stories of addiction—and recovery—honestly and openly.

My experience is that men can love God and porn at the same time. I see it every week. I know these men and they know me. But again, I can only speak for myself.

A PHYSIOLOGICAL RESPONSE

One of the great benefits of attaining my master's degree in addiction recovery was the study of the physiology of sex addiction. This space does not allow for an extensive discussion on the subject, but I will hit a couple of high points.

There are several contributors to sex addiction. A person doesn't decide to be an addict. There are many contributing causes, such as abnormal levels of sex hormones and chemicals in the brain, such as dopamine. There are brain abnormalities, childhood abuse, and emotional trauma. Emerging data suggest a correlation between porn addiction and OCD, alcoholism, and eating disorders.

On average, a person is first exposed to porn by age 11, usually not by choice. And rarely is early exposure to porn just a onetime occurrence. This triggers a neurological response that begins a journey of no return. Neuropsychologist Dr. Tim Jennings says it like this: "Any type of repetitive behavior will create trails in our brain that are going to fire on an automatic sequence."[4]

Dr. Bob Hughes, a clinical psychologist, says his views of sex addiction have evolved as he has studied the compulsion and treated thousands of patients. He now describes sex addiction as both a sinful choice and a biological disease. He says a series of poor sexual choices becomes "an addiction which can grab onto a person and rob him of his volition."[5]

The result for many men and women is years of unsolicited bondage. That is why 62 percent of men can love God enough to be in church every Sunday while still struggling with porn. They love God with all their hearts, but they are trapped in sexual bondage. The cycle is hard to break. To whom do they turn? They certainly can't stand up in most Sunday school classes and say, "Hi, my name is Larry, and I'm a sexaholic." So the struggle continues. Their repeated use of porn has literally changed the physical structure of their brains.

We know that 81 percent of sex addicts were abused as children—and zero percent of them

4   Luke Gibbons, "Porn Trends," World Magazine, Vol. 30, No. 20. (October 3, 2015).

5   Gibbons, "Porn Trends," World Magazine, Vol. 30, No. 20. (October 3, 2015).

chose that abuse. But in every case, this sets the brain on a course that isn't good.

Every CSAT (certified sex addiction therapist) will confirm that sex addiction is an intimacy disorder. It is often triggered in the brain by isolation. This comes in many forms. When we isolate as children, we are at risk. It was not until I got into serious recovery that I realized how my own isolation contributed to my addiction. As a young child, bones in my lower legs had not formed correctly, so I wore painful leg braces. This limited my physical activity so I couldn't play with the other children in my neighborhood. By the age of eight, I was legally blind (20/200), which meant wearing the biggest, thickest horn-rimmed glasses of any third grader alive.

On top of that, I stuttered until I was 15—not horribly, but enough to get laughed at daily. So what did I do? I sat in the back of every class, avoided speaking at all costs, got picked last for every team at recess, and had few friends. I hated going to school. I was alone. And I was a sitting duck for sex addiction—though I could have never seen it coming.

Are porn and sex addiction a moral issue or a physiological issue? Yes. Sex addicts do not choose their addiction. But they do choose what they do about it. And unfortunately, because the road to recovery is difficult, long, and marked by unexpected turns, it is a road not traveled enough. There are cliffs to either side of the road, and the traveler can lose his sobriety with just one bad turn or choice.

Porn addiction is a physiological problem. When exposed to alcohol, nicotine, caffeine, chocolate, or porn—whether by choice or not—the journey toward addiction begins. Toss in abuse and isolation, and the surprise is not that so many are addicted to porn but that so many are finding recovery.

So physiology and neurology give us an answer. A man can love God and porn at the same time.

A THEOLOGICAL RESPONSE

I am interested in what Patrick Carnes, Mark Laaser, Doug Weiss, and Stephen Arterburn have to say about sex addiction. I am interested in what my spouse has to say, what my sponsor has to say, and what you have to say. But mostly, I am interested in what God has to say about porn and sex addiction. I want a biblical response to my condition. Because my theology is rooted in Scripture, it is there that I must turn. I offer a five-point theological response to addiction.

1. WE ARE ALL BORN INTO SIN.

We are sinners because we sin. But the opposite is also true. We sin because we are sinners. For the porn addict, the root of his problem is not his family of origin, but original sin. The psalmist declared, "I was brought forth in sin. And in sin my mother conceived me" (Psalm 51:5). Paul wrote, "In me nothing good dwells" (Romans 7:18). Whether addicts or not, we all share this in common—we were all born into sin.

2. SIN IS BOTH A CONDITION AND A CHOICE.

That great theologian Mark Twain wrote, "Adam was but human—this explains it all. He didn't want the apple for the apple's sake. He wanted it only because it was forbidden."[6] Adam craved the "apple" for a variety of reasons. But even the most intriguing temptation didn't override his free choice. No matter the height of a person's addiction, no matter how great his temptation, every

---

6   Mark Twain, www.twainquotes.com/Adam.html.

slip, relapse, or fall is the result of his personal choice. The addict must own his disease. Is it fair for the addict to ask, "Why was I the one abused as a child? Why was I the one who found his father's porn stash at age twelve? Why was I the one whose parents demonstrated no affection? Why did I fall into an addiction I deplore?" Yes, all those questions are fair game. But an addict's addiction is no excuse for a single act of sexual impurity. Sin is a condition, but it is also a choice.

3. STRUGGLE WITH SIN NEVER GOES AWAY.

Let's consider the struggle of Paul. His story is told in Romans 7. From the passages below, notice the intensity of his personal frustration and pain.

"I do not understand what I do. For what I want to do I do not do, but what I hate to do" (7:15).

"In me nothing good dwells" (7:18).

"I have the desire to do what is good, but I cannot carry it out" (7:18).

"I do not the good I want to do, but the evil I do not want to do—this I keep on doing. Now if I do what I do not want to do, it is no longer I who do it, but it is sin living in me that does it" (7:19-20).

"Wretched man that I am!" (7:24).

The struggle with sin never goes away. For the addict, his temptation is a reliable companion, his most enduring unwanted partner. Luther coined the Latin phrase—*simul Justus et peccator*—simultaneously righteous and sinner. Paul was both saint and sinner at the same time. To repeat J.I. Packer, "Paul wasn't struggling with sin because he was such a sinner. Paul was struggling with sin because he was such a saint."[7]

Paul fought the temptations of sin. He found himself doing what he didn't want to do and not doing what he should. He wanted to do right but often fell short of that goal. Paul confessed his own ignorance. "I don't understand what I do" (7:15). I count dozens of porn and sex addicts among my circle of friends. I talk to some of them every day. Most of them battle their addiction with all of their might and power. Sometimes they fail. More often they succeed. But always, they keep on fighting.

In his classic exposition on the Book of Romans, Donald Barnhouse wrote, "The believer in

---

[7] Kenneth Berding, A Key Insight about Romans 7 from a Conversation with J.I. Packer. (La Mirada, CA: Biola University, April 4, 2012).

Christ is given power to overcome the outbreaks of Adamic nature, but its presence constantly contaminates his life on earth."[8] Like the porn addict, Paul struggled, but he never gave up. And it was in that struggle that he proved the strength of his faith. An addict need not feel shame over his addiction; the real shame is when he quits trying to overcome.

4. WHILE WE MAY NOT KNOW FREEDOM FROM ADDICTION, WE CAN KNOW FREEDOM IN ADDICTION.

Jude wrote of a God "who is able to keep you from stumbling" (Jude 24). Notice he didn't promise that God would keep us from struggling. Many times, we ask God to take us out of the storm when his better plan is to take us through it. Before coming to Christ, we lived under the penalty of sin. Now we wrestle with the power of sin. There will come a time when we will be freed from the presence of sin.

A true Christ-follower knows the struggle of sin. Luther said, "Be a sinner and sin strongly, but

---

8   Donald Grey Barnhouse, Romans. (Grand Rapids, MI: Eerdmans, 1983).

more strongly have faith and rejoice in Christ."[9] The addict must not abandon his faith. Matthew Henry summarized Paul's struggle with sin: "Paul could not deliver himself; none of us can."[10] It is when we accept our condition that we find freedom.

5. WHAT GOD ALLOWS TODAY, HE WILL USE TOMORROW.

Charles Stanley writes, "The scars of sin can lead us to restoration and a renewed intimacy with God."[11] John Wesley said, "Give me one hundred preachers who fear nothing but sin and desire nothing but God."[12] A truism I learned several years ago is that what God allows, he redeems. He will use my addiction—if I let him.

One of the great tragedies of the modern church is its reluctance to address the crisis of sex

---

9 "Martin Luther Quotes that Still Ring True," Relevant Magazine (October 31, 2017). http://relevantmagazine. com/god/ 18-martin-luther-quotes-still-ring-true.

10 Matthew Henry, Matthew Henry, Commentary on the Whole Bible. (Grand Rapids, MI: Zondervan Publishing, 1961).

11 www.amazon.com/When-learn-experience -scars-Charles/dp/BO1MOHTCJ7.

12 Lauren Porter, "Give Me One Hundred Preachers," Porter's Progress (April 23, 2010). http://laurenporter. wordpress.com /2010/04/23/give-me-one-hundred-preachers/.

addiction. I've never heard of a man who was ostra-cized from the church or even the pastorate because of a "proud look." Yet, "proud look" heads the list of the seven deadly sins listed in Scripture (Proverbs 6:16–19). Pope Gregory updated the list in 600 A.D. to include pride, greed, lust, envy, gluttony, wrath, and sloth. When's the last time you saw a church leader in the news because he ate too much?

None of this is to justify sex or porn addiction. There is no excuse for acting out. None. Ever. But what God allows, he can use. I have seen broken marriages restored and shattered lives put back to-gether again. But first, we must seek our redemp-tion in Christ. John Piper was right when he said, "God is most glorified in us when we are most sat-isfied in him."[13]

Every morning I pray the Third Step Prayer that is familiar to many addicts. It's a great way to start any day, and it is my theological response to my addiction: "God, I offer myself to you, to build with me and do with me as you will. Relieve me of the bondage of self, that I may better do your will. Take away my difficulties that I may bear witness

_____

13   John Piper, Desiring God. (Sermon delivered October 13, 2012). http://www.desiringgod. org/.../god-is-most-glorified-in-us-whenwe-are-most-satisfied.

to those I would help of your power, your love, and your way of life."

A PREDICTIVE RESPONSE

What does all this mean going forward? I predict three things. First, with the explosion of technology, sex and porn addiction will only get worse—a lot worse.

Second, Christian leaders will be increasingly vulnerable, as they isolate, lack personal accountability, and know their churches view porn as a sin too great to forgive. For too many pastors, to stand up and say "I'm struggling with porn" is the same thing as "Please toss me to the curb." Out of personal embarrassment, disgrace, and the fear of losing their jobs clergy will too often not seek the help they need.

Third, the church will begin to respond to the issues of sex and porn addiction in a healthy way— slowly. With every pastor's fall from grace, with more recovering addicts telling their stories, the church will awaken to this issue. It is already happening, just not very quickly. But I predict that SA will become the new AA. In 20–30 years, the church will have an adequate, redemptive, grace-focused, restorative response to the issue. At least, that is my prayer.

A person can love God and porn at the same time. If I didn't believe that, I wouldn't be in recovery myself. If I didn't believe that, Beth and I wouldn't be telling our stories. Because we believe the answer is "Yes!," we formed this ministry and gave it the name that has kept us going through decades of struggle, addiction, and despair—There's Still Hope.

What are the Components of Recovery?

Recovery is both a gift and a reward. It is a gift from God, for without him we cannot find sobriety. And it is a reward because without us God will not grant sobriety. Without him, we can't; without us, God won't.

But how do we break the cycle of addiction, exactly? Speaking in generalities, we must rely on God as our Higher Power. We need the structure and tested paradigm provided by the twelve steps. Rarely does a person find sobriety apart from personal therapy. It is best to seek the services of a CSAT when possible. But here let's identify the four key components of successful recovery.

The biblical model I will use is that of John 5:1-15. It's the story of the paralytic who had been sick for 38 years. His miracle of restoration is a template for every kind of addict. This is his story.

On his way to a Jewish festival, Jesus saw the unnamed man by a small body of water just outside of Jerusalem. The blind, lame, and paralyzed came to this place daily, desperate for the healing powers that legend tied to this pool. This particular invalid somehow caught Jesus' eye.

Never one to forsake the individual for the sake of the crowd, Jesus confronted the man with the strangest of questions. "Do you want to be well?" (John 5:6).

Jesus paused to allow the man to explain that he had exhausted all possibilities. Where the doctors had failed him, the supposed healing waters of the pool were his last chance. But he confessed that this had also left him lame and frustrated.

Then Jesus told him, "Get up! Pick up your mat and walk" (5:8). Could he finally walk again–after 38 years? The next move was his.

"At once the man was cured; he picked up his mat and walked" (5:9). The man did what only he could do (pick up his mat). Then Jesus did what only he could do (heal the man). It was at the moment that the man did the improbable that Jesus did the impossible.

Fast forward five verses. "Later Jesus found him at the temple and said to him, 'See, you are well again. Stop sinning or something worse may happen to you.' The man went away and told the Jewish leaders that it was Jesus who had made him well" (5:14-15).

In this remarkable story, we uncover the four components to every story of successful recovery. First, the paralytic was desperate. Jesus asked him if he really wanted to be well. Was he willing to go to any measure to find restoration?

Second, there had to be surrender. Notice, Jesus didn't do all he could do until after the man did all he could do. Jesus told him to pick up his mat—which did not require healing. He could do that laying down. But it made no sense. "Why pick up my mat?" he must have thought. "Because I said to," Jesus would have replied. In early recovery, we are often asked to do things that don't quite make sense: going to meetings, telling our story, getting a sponsor. But healing is all about surrender, which means doing what may not make sense in the moment.

Third, recovery required community. One day, Jesus healed the man. The next time he saw him was at church. There was something deep inside the man that screamed out for community. The healing (sobriety) was the gift of God, but his lasting strength (recovery) would depend largely on his fellowship with others.

Fourth, the man made a disclosure. "The man went away and told the Jewish leaders that it was Jesus who had made him well" (5:15). There is something magical that happens when we tell our story to others. That is what the 12th step is all about. Disclosure was a part of the paralytic's story; it must also be a part of yours.

That is just one man's story. You have your own. But as with the paralytic, your story of recovery will always include these four components.

Let's dig a little deeper.

DESPERATION

Recovery is not for the faint of heart. Half-baked measures will not suffice. Unfortunately, most of us prefer the problem we know over the solution we don't. We want recovery; we just aren't so sure about the process of recovery. I have yet to meet the man who said, "I am happy to live in my addiction. It has really worked out well for me." I've heard a lot of stories in the hundreds of 12-step meetings I've attended. But I'm still waiting for the story that begins, "I was tempted to act out. I gave in, and I'm sure glad I did."

So why don't more people get into recovery? It's simple. They aren't desperate—yet. And it's understandable. To the addict, his habit has become his most reliable friend. Where he goes, it goes. It never leaves him alone. It lives inside his head. It brings relief when called upon while making no demands.

Why is it that most people have to "hit bottom" before they really commit to the process of recovery? Because they must be desperate. And until we hit bottom, we are not desperate.

Before you ask God to heal you, ask him to make you desperate. Be like the man who said, "The day my wife discovered my addiction was the worst day of my life—and the best."

The Bible is full of men who submitted to life change but only after a crisis that birthed desperation deep within their spirits. Recovery came to Moses—after he had killed a man. Recovery came to Samson—after he lost all his strength. Recovery came to David—after he was punished for adultery. Recovery came to Elijah—after he nearly died of hunger. Recovery came to Jonah—after three days in the belly of a fish. Recovery came to Peter—after he heard the rooster's crow.

Recovery can be your greatest gift, but only if you are willing to go to any length to unwrap it. Jesus' question from 2,000 years ago has echoed through the chambers of time. It is his foundational question for every addict. "Do you want to get well?"

SURRENDER

Living in one's addiction is a matter of control. Addicts want to control their circumstances, moods, pleasures, and other people. But they cannot control themselves. It is only when we recognize that we have a problem that we cannot solve that we are ready for recovery. Only then are we likely to turn to God.

Dwight L. Moody said, "Let God have your life; he can do more with it than you can." Only through surrender can we make the right choices.[14] A. W.

---

14   www.inspirationalchristians.org/biography/dwight-l-moody-biography.

Tozer wrote, "The man or woman who is wholly surrendered to Christ can't make a wrong choice—any choice will be the right one."[15] Any successful road to recovery begins with surrender. Every day I tell myself, "I'm not saying I'll never act out again, but I am saying it won't happen today." Then I pray the Third Step prayer of surrender.

Finding sobriety is not about trying harder. Telling an addict to try harder only tightens the noose of bondage. When we tell men to just pray harder, try harder, and love Jesus more, it is like telling a crippled man to try harder to walk. We add shame to guilt. The problem is not lack of effort, but surrender. The Bible says, "The Spirit [not our own human effort] enables us to deny the flesh and resist temptation" (Romans 8:14). With surrender, a new pattern develops (Titus 2:11–12). Surrender is the first component of recovery.

COMMUNITY

Recovery is a team sport. I have never met a person who found sobriety in isolation. Michael Leahy, the founder of *BraveHearts* addiction ministry,

---

15   George Sweeting, Who Said That? (Chicago: Moody Publishers, 1995).

says that only one in 10,000 finds successful recovery in isolation. In fact, it is that isolation that actually drives a man into addiction in the first place. The problem cannot be the cure. For a man to try to find sobriety on his own would be as suicidal as washing down poison with more poison. The *AA Big Book* says, "The feeling of having shared in a common peril is one element in the powerful cement which binds us."[16]

Jesus set the example for healthy growth and boundaries. He was committed to community. He spent three years with twelve men, and even more time with three of the twelve. But notice, though he called men to a personal relationship with him, he never called them to a private relationship with him.

The Book of James gives excellent insight to the necessity of community: "Confess your sins one to another, that you may be healed" (James 5:16). That is stunning. James did not say, "Confess your sins to God." He said to confess your sins to "one another." The purpose of confession in a small group, James said, is healing. And that is the goal of every

---

16 Alcoholics Anonymous, 4th ed. (New York, NY: Alcoholics Anonymous World Services, Inc., 2002), 17.

addict—healing. Apart from community there is no healing.

A great place to start is by joining a 12-step group. Dr. Doug Weiss, author of *The Final Freedom: Pioneering Sexual Addiction Recovery*, suggests recovery must be tailored to the individual addict. But he is an advocate for, "in most cases, a personal accountability partner and weekly group meetings." He writes, "I have never met anyone who has experienced sexual addiction recovery alone."[17]

DISCLOSURE

This is the one I fought the hardest. Early in recovery, I was okay with surrender to God. I embraced 12-step work. But disclosure is where I drew the line. I wasn't ready to tell my story—at least not to my wife. But Mark Laaser is right when he says, "Silence is the greatest enemy of sexual health."[18]

There are three levels of disclosure. The first level is partial disclosure. With that, the addict tells his or her spouse what he or she has to tell them. The addict has been caught; it's time to come clean.

---

17 Doug Weiss, "What Is Sex Addiction?" (Heart to Heart Counseling Center).
18 Mark Laaser, Talking to Your Kids About Sex. (Colorado Springs, CO: WaterBrook Press, 1999).

But because the addict is not coming clean of his or her own will, there is natural resistance. So the addict tells the spouse a little more than the spouse already knows, thinking, "This will satisfy them." Partial disclosure is the same thing as gradual disclosure—telling the wounded partner a little of one's story at a time. And there has never been a wounded spouse who preferred it this way. It's torturous. But it's what addicts do. We are liars. We tell only what we have to. Every addict starts at this level of disclosure.

The second level of disclosure is a full, nonclinical disclosure. This is a written disclosure in which the addict reads his story to his wife in the presence of a counselor. He gets the whole story out. And then his spouse has the opportunity to respond. This is normally done in one, long counseling session.

The third level of disclosure is a full clinical disclosure. This is best done as part of a three-day intensive with a trained CSAT. The addict reads his story to his wife in the presence of the therapist. Then she responds with a series of questions. This is followed by a full polygraph examination. The purpose of the polygraph is to determine whether the addict has been entirely forthcoming.

I am a huge proponent of a full clinical disclosure for three reasons. First, it finally paints the whole picture for the wounded spouse. Wives want honesty above all else. They need to know what they are dealing with in their husband's addiction. It is the fear of the unknown that haunts them the most. Second, it gives the marriage a reset. From that moment forward, the past is left in the past. Further questions about the addict's past will no longer be entertained. This gives the addict an indescribable feeling of hope and restoration. And third, a full disclosure reprograms the addict's mind toward honestly.

I resisted doing a full clinical disclosure myself. But Beth insisted. Eventually, I agreed, and what resulted was the first absolute, honest expression of my hurts, habits, and hang-ups (Celebrate Recovery language) she had ever heard from me. I have done three follow-up one-day clinical disclosures since—each with a fresh polygraph exam. (I have passed each polygraph exam.) I don't do this because Beth asks me to, but because I want to. I want her to experience the peace of mind that comes from knowing I am sober, free, and honest—a peace of mind I robbed from her for so many years.

Debra Laaser, co-leader of *Faithful and True Ministries*, recommends a full disclosure up front, early in recovery. "Knowing the whole truth is foundational to building a new life together because the new structure must be built on honesty and openness."[19]

To couples who aren't sure they want to do a full clinical disclosure (with polygraph), I say, "Why not?" If the addict is truly clean, and if he or she has genuinely told all of his or her story, that addict should want the spouse to know it as close to 100 percent as possible. If you are the wounded spouse, by accepting anything less than a polygraph you are assuming your spouse—who has lied to you for years—is suddenly going to share with you his deepest secrets and darkest moments. And you will always have at least a hint of a doubt.

In fact, we believe in the full disclosure with polygraph so strongly that There's Still Hope grants scholarships. We will fund $100 of your first polygraph if done within the context of a three-day intensive through our ministry or with a trained CSAT.

---

19   Debbie Laaser, http://faithfulandtrue. com/product/full-disclosure.

How Can the Church Effectively Respond?

Stuart Vogelman, executive director of *Pure Warrior Ministries*, says, "The church is going to have to decide if it's going to fight to be the pure bride of Christ. It's probably going to be the toughest battle the church has ever faced, and most churches are not equipped for it."[20] Even though porn and sex addiction are ravaging the lives of men in the church, including her leaders, her muted response has been deafening. Josh McDowell has released a survey which confirms this: only nine percent of church attendees and seven percent of pastors say their church has a program or response to this

---

20 Stuart Vogelman (Pure Warrior Ministries). www.prweb. com/releases/2006/04/prweb368551.htm.

growing problem. We suggest seven steps toward a comprehensive response by the local church.

RECOGNIZE THE MAGNITUDE OF THE PROBLEM

According to the *National Institute of Health*, 2.2 million Americans use wheelchairs. That represents .7 percent of the population. *The Hearing Loss Association of America* reports that 15 percent of American adults have some level of hearing loss. One study concludes that only 3.1 percent of commercial buildings (including churches) will ever have a significant fire (VTT Publications).

So, let's consider a church of 500 in attendance. Statistically, they will have only four who need a wheelchair, but they still have wheelchair accommodations. They will have only 45 who have hearing loss (15 percent of the adults), but they still have devices for the hearing impaired. And they have fire extinguishers, even though there is a 97 percent chance they will never be needed.

This same church trains several members to perform CPR and provides a costly automated external defibrillator (AED) in case of cardiac arrest, despite the slim chances this will ever be used.

Now let's talk about the church's response to porn addiction. While .7 percent of her men need wheelchair ramps, 15 percent need hearing assistance, and very few will ever need fire protection or heart treatment at the church, 62 percent of them struggle with porn (Proven Men).

So the church of 500 has about 150 men. One of those 150 men needs a wheelchair ramp. But 93 of those men need help with their porn use and compulsive sexual activity. Still, only seven percent of pastors have put in place a response to this significant challenge.

Still not convinced we have a problem? Let me repeat: 37 percent of pastors struggle with porn (*Christianity Today*), 53 percent viewed porn after attending a *Promise Keepers* event (*Barna*), 50 percent of the church struggles with cybersex (*Covenant Eyes*), and 18 percent of the men in church admit they are or might be addicted to sex (*Church-Militant.com*).

The first step for the addict is to recognize the problem. The first response for the church is the same.

APPOINT AND TRAIN AN ADDICTION MINISTRY LEADER

If your church has any members, you need an addiction recovery leader. You won't survive the twenty-first century without one. This person may be on staff, perhaps over men's ministry. They will more likely be a layperson. The good news is that training is available. *Celebrate Recovery* offers excellent one-day conferences around the country that train volunteers to lead addiction recovery ministries. *Celebrate Recovery* addresses "hurts, habits, and hang-ups," and therefore offers a wide response to addiction needs. This is helpful as a comprehensive church addiction recovery ministry will need to address more than sex addiction. Substance abuse recovery will need to be a part of any comprehensive ministry, so your leader will need training in more than sex addiction recovery.

The leader need not be an expert in addiction recovery. She is a facilitator who should coordinate the ministry. This will include offering tools that are already available. This person will need to organize and lead the details of this ministry as follows.

CREATE A CULTURE OF REDEMPTION

No effective addiction recovery ministry ca
survive apart from a culture of redemption. All
dicts who go to church know the Bible verses that
condemn their behavior. Paul said, "Put to death
what is earthly in you: sexual immorality, impurity,
passion, evil desire" (Colossians 3:5). But the same
God who inspired that Scripture also demonstrated
grace toward the woman caught in adultery.

Remember, addicts live in isolation. Secre-
cy feeds the addiction. Addicts need a place to go
and a person to whom they can turn. But sex addicts don't tell anyone about their disease for three
sad, but legitimate reasons: they think they are all
alone, they fear being judged, and they feel enor-
mous shame. Even after years of healthy recovery,
I rarely introduce myself to a new friend by saying,
"Hi! I'm Mark, and I'm a sexaholic!"

Your church must be seen as a safe environ-
ment for those who struggle the most. I will be for-
ever grateful for the brothers in Christ who have
embraced me despite my addiction and whose love
for me was not and is not conditional. Unless your
church exudes a culture of redemption, you don't
have a chance to minister effectively to the 62

percent of your men who viewed porn last month. You don't need to tell them they are bad. They already believe that. What they need to hear is that God is good.

START MEN'S AND WOMEN'S GROUPS

Offer frequent small groups that address the deepest needs of men and women. And I suggest real discipleship is rarely done in mixed-sex groups. If you could best do small groups by putting men and women together, Jesus would have tried that. The fact is—like it or not—men and women will not feel comfortable sharing their most intimate struggles in a room populated by the opposite sex. In fact, many SA and SAA groups don't even allow for mixed-sex groups.

A great place to start for men is with an *Every Man's Battle* small group. Recognize that addicts and those who may be addicts need a safe place to go to learn and share their struggles. Telling someone to just pray more about their problem is like telling someone to put out a forest fire with a squirt gun. I know a minister who attends 12-step meetings every week under an alias, to protect his identity. When he told a few other ministers about his struggles, they told him to pray more. He told me, "What they didn't understand was that my problem wasn't with prayer, it was with porn."

To find recovery, the men and women in your church need more small groups and less condemnation. There is safety in small groups. I attend a weekly men's group (not focused on addiction). We share our greatest struggles. I've been in this group for three years. I try to never miss. I wouldn't trade this group of guys for anything in the world.

HOST 12-STEP GROUPS

Make your church available for 12-step groups such as *Celebrate Recovery*. Many churches host *AA* meetings. As a regular attendee of two *SA* (Sexaholics Anonymous) groups and a past member of several *SAA* (Sex Addicts Anonymous) groups, I can attest to their significant role in recovery. Every Christian counselor I know recommends these groups to their clients. They are spiritual programs.

Many *SA* and *SAA* groups struggle to find a home. Churches need to step forward. These groups raise their own funds and are self-supporting so they can pay a small fee for the use of a church facility.

Hosting 12-step meetings will do two things. First, it will help those in recovery. Second, it will be a witness to your community—that you are there for them. I have a pastor friend whose church mantra is "The Church for Messed-Up People." That should be all of our churches. So go ahead. Host a group. And in the process, don't forget the spouse. In addition to offering an *SA* or *SAA* group a place to meet, remember the *S-ANON* group. This is for spouses of sex addicts. By providing space for meetings for both the addict and the spouse, you will minister to the whole family.

SPONSOR ANNUAL EVENTS

Your church can offer a specific, creative response to your men and women who suffer. For example, you should provide an annual event like a men's Saturday breakfast called "Pancakes and Porn," through our ministry. Make sure your pastor and staff support the event. One church in the Dallas area had over 200 men attend such an event.

You should also provide information for protecting electronic devices from the trappings of porn. Covenant Eyes and Ever Accountable provide excellent protection. Other helpful ideas include putting out recovery literature, doing interviews with recovering addicts during church services, and promoting area recovery events.

PROVIDE ADDICTION COUNSELING

If you cannot provide addiction counseling at your church, at least know where people can find such help. Be a resource for those who suffer. But keep in mind, porn addiction counseling requires specialized training. When possible, refer people to a local certified sex addiction therapist (CSAT) trained to respond to the physiological, emotional, and relational needs of their clients. There are now about 4,000 such trained therapists, so in most metropolitan areas you will find at least one.

Because specialized therapy is more expensive, provide financial assistance if possible. For couples ready for real healing, we strongly recommend a three-day intensive with a clinical disclosure that includes a polygraph. This is a cornerstone to lasting recovery. Nothing will set a couple on the path of healing more quickly and successfully than a three-day intensive.

WHAT ABOUT PORN IN THE PULPIT?

I recently read the story of a pastor who struggled with porn. He turned to his denominational hierarchy for help. In an anonymous letter, he wrote, "I consider myself a good person who happens to be suffering from sex addiction." His supervisor responded in writing: "You are not a good person, but a bad one."

This is what faces most clergy who suffer from porn or sex addiction—shame and helplessness. A plumber or auto technician can seek help without losing their job; a pastor likely cannot. When discovered, even if he is already in recovery, the minister is often kicked to the curb. He is defined by his addiction.

As already stated, only seven percent of churches have any plan in place to address the problem of porn in the pew; almost none have a response to porn in the pulpit. While each church and faith group needs to formulate its own plan, we hope this will provide a template for consideration. We will frame our response to the issue of porn in the pulpit by addressing five fundamental questions.

HOW BIG IS THE PROBLEM?

Though most churches would be astonished to find that there is porn in their pulpit, the data is clear. In simple terms, the typical church with two ministers on staff has porn in their pulpit. While different surveys produce variant statistics, the magnitude of the problem is indisputable.

- Fifty-four percent of pastors viewed porn last year. (*Pastors.com*)
- Sixty-three percent of pastors struggle with sexual compulsion or masturbation. (Patrick Means, *Men's Secret Wars*)
- Fifty-seven percent of pastors and 64 percent of student pastors have struggled with porn. (*Barna*)
- Thirty-seven percent of pastors struggle with porn. (*Christianity Today*)

- Twenty-five percent of pastors have purchased porn. (*Barna*)
- Fifteen percent of pastors are struggling "right now." (*Barna*)
- Eighty-seven percent of pastors who use porn feel great shame over it. (*OneNewsNow.com*)
- Fifty-five percent of pastors who use porn live in constant fear of being discovered. (*OneNewsNow.com*)
- Seventy percent of pastors who call the Focus on the Family toll-free helpline claim to be addicted to porn.
- Seventy-five percent of pastors have no accountability for their time or behavior. (Patrick Means)

WHY DO PASTORS STRUGGLE WITH PORN?

Pastors are perhaps the most susceptible to the attack of porn and sex addiction for several reasons. While it is impossible to know all the contributing factors to porn in the pulpit, several jump out.

First, pastors are the natural target of the enemy. Satan knows that if he brings down the pastor, he will harm the church. We can all think of examples where this has proven true. The senior pastor is the most natural target of enemy attack. It is a spiritual issue.

Second, pastors live on pedestals. They enjoy the rush of speaking before large crowds every week (admittedly, captive audiences), hearing lots of praise, and living in an age that has built a wall between clergy and laity. As one speaker said, "The church has sanitized her pastor." It's not that pastors fall more than others, it is just more noticed, for the higher the pedestal, the greater the fall.

Third, pastors isolate. They have little accountability and spend hours alone, unmonitored, each week. When they "visit the hospitals," no one really knows where they are the entire time. Adding to their isolation is that no one in the church can really understand the pressures a pastor feels until they have been there. His job is never done; the stress is tremendous. That is why, according to Dr. John Bisagno, only one in ten pastors finishes strong.

Fourth, ministers are relational by nature. They need to be. But this makes them more susceptible to affairs and inappropriate behavior. Their position and demeanor make pastors more attractive to women than they would otherwise be, as women are largely relationally and emotionally centered.

Fifth, pastors receive more criticism than most professionals. As a result, they become people pleasers. Their drive for approval leads many pastors to indulge in artificial relationships with porn or even prostitutes. These relationships place no demands on the addict, and in that sense, they are safe.

Sixth, pastors feel bulletproof. Because there is little accountability, the minister can live in his addiction for years without being discovered. And with every passing day, he comes to assume that since he has not been caught, he will not be caught. "God will protect me," he reasons. Some go so far in their thinking as to assume God is under an obligation to protect them, simply for the sake of the church.

So what is the answer? Both the church and pastor bear responsibility. The church needs to be a redemptive fellowship that is safe even for her leaders. And the pastor needs to live a confessional life. I like the way Tal Prince says it: "The pastor needs to lead with a limp."[21] By presenting himself

---

21   Tal Prince, "Leading with a Limp," Internet Pornography: A Ministry Leader's Handbook, 2010. http://

as not only a saint but also a struggler, the pastor becomes real.

WHAT BOUNDARIES CAN BE PUT IN PLACE?

Andy Stanley's great study *Guardrails* suggests that we all need to put up guardrails to keep ourselves out of the ditches of life. A guardrail, Stanley notes, is put up in the safe zone in order to keep traffic out of the ditch.

What are some guardrails pastors can put up in a noble effort to maintain personal purity?

First, a pastor should never be alone with any women other than his wife. The only exception would be a counseling session with a woman (and even this is questionable) in which case the pastor's assistant is just outside his office. This guardrail applies to lunches away from the church building. The pastor should not be alone with a woman in his car, either. This invites temptation and spurs gossip, at the least.

Second, ministers should install glass windows into their office doors or leave their doors open at

wagmunacom/flash/downloads/Covenant-Eyes-Internet-Porn.

all times. The point is not that outsiders look in, but that they know they can. Again, this supplies the pastor with another layer of accountability.

Third, the pastor needs a small group with whom he can share anything. He needs to be able to say to another man, in confidence, "I am struggling with lust." Solomon said, "As iron sharpens iron, so one man sharpens another" (Proverbs 27:17). The pastor needs men to whom he can confess his greatest struggles. Remember, James said healing comes by confessing our sins to each other, not just to God (James 5:16).

Fourth, a block should be put on the minister's computer, cutting off accessibility to porn sites. In *Out of the Shadows*, Patrick Carnes writes, "There are now people struggling with sexual compulsivity who never would have been if not for the Internet."[22] A highly effective tool is provided by Covenant Eyes, which sends a weekly report to an accountability partner, notifying him of any questionable content that has been accessed.

---

22   Patrick Carnes, Out of the Shadows. (Center City, MN: Hazelden Publishing, 3rd ed., 2001).

TO WHOM ARE PASTORS ACCOUNTABLE?

Dennis Swanberg contributes to this discussion with his book, *The Man Code*. He suggests each of us needs to follow the pattern of Scripture by intentionally participating in certain groups as enumerated in the New Testament, such as one (God), 12 (small group), 120 (the church), and 3,000 (community). But Dennis also emphasizes the need for a small accountability group of three, just as Jesus related to Peter, James, and John on a unique level.

God calls each of us, including the pastor, into a personal relationship with his Son. But as we have noted, he did not call any of us into a private relationship with his Son. Mark Laaser suggests that in early recovery, each addict requires daily accountability as well as weekly support groups. He says, "One guy is not enough."[23]

Who should these three men be for the struggling pastor? Some suggest he turn to a fellow staff member. I feel this is a mistake, as this can blur the professional relationship among the church staff. Another option would be long-distance

---

23 Mark Laaser, "7 Principles of Highly Accountable Men." http://www.christian book.com/7-principles-of-highlyaccountable-men.

relationships. Developing close ties to a few local pastors might be an excellent option, but these relationships must be entered into with care. Trust usually takes a lot of time to develop. Some choose to build their closest, most confessional relationships with men in their church. All I can say is to proceed slowly and with caution.

WHAT IF THE PASTOR FALLS?

Again, very few churches have a plan in place. The result is that they must deal with the most traumatic crisis imaginable with zero planning. That is a huge mistake. The best response is preemptive, meaning it is wise to create the boundaries and redemptive culture that will best protect both the pastor and the church. Then it is critical to remember the issue is not if your pastor struggles with porn, but when. Since roughly one-half of all ministers share this struggle, your church likely has a minister on staff who is struggling with porn right now.

Let's assume two things happen. First, your pastor is struggling or has struggled with porn or sex addiction. Second, this has been discovered.

Now, what do you do as a church? We suggest several guiding principles.

1. THINK REDEMPTIVELY.

This does not mean that every pastor should keep his position in the church after he is discovered. But the fundamental principle that should guide every response to a pastor's fall, no matter how egregious, is redemption. You may not redeem his position, but that should never be the primary goal, anyway. It is about redeeming the man. Perhaps it will help if you remember his problem is one of the head and not the heart. I've never heard of a pastor who wants to be a sex addict. They feel more shame than any other addict—more than you can imagine. Jesus said, "A battered reed he [God] will not break off, and a smoldering wick he will not put out" (Matthew 12:20). In other words, God still has a plan for the fallen pastor. There is nothing he could ever do to make God love him more, and nothing he has ever done has made God love him less.

2. RESPOND BIBLICALLY.

It is a grave mistake to respond to a pastor's failings as though we didn't have a Bible to guide us. The church is unlike any other institution in the world. The Bible is our handbook. So when you respond to a pastor's sin, consult the handbook. (Better yet, have a biblical plan already in place.) There are several Scriptures you need to wrestle with. The pastor is to be "above reproach" (1 Timothy 3:2). The Bible also says, "There is forgiveness with God" (Psalm 130:4). The question of whether a pastor can be returned to his position following his discovery is informed by many factors: whether he was already in recovery when he was discovered, whether he had an affair with someone in the church, whether he used church funds to pay for his habit, and whether he is truly repentant and willing to go to any length to get well. Each church must answer these questions based on its own heritage and interpretation of the Scriptures.

3. REACT COMPASSIONATELY.

Sadly, when most pastors fall they are confronted by a few men in the church, forced to resign, instructed to not return to the church, and then completely abandoned. They are written out of the church history, treated as though their tenure at the church (and all the good things they achieved) never happened, and kicked to the curb.

The church ends all contact with them, apart from a small severance.

Remember, church, the world is your audience. They are watching you! There are a few examples of churches where the pastor was discovered in the height of his addiction, and properly removed from his position, but with time was restored to the fellowship, if not his position. The church walked with him—and his family—through their darkest valley.

Church—do not abandon your pastor or his wife! They suddenly have no job, probably have to move, and are scared. While it is true that his sin has found him out (Numbers 32:23), grace needs to find him as well. So when you react to your pastor's fall, keep a few things in mind. Remember how Jesus dealt with the woman caught in adultery—and with her accusers. Remember that the same Peter who denied even knowing Jesus was sent out just a few weeks later to preach the most important sermon in the history of Christianity.

4. PROVIDE FINANCIALLY.

Your pastor now needs a job. He will likely need to move. This means his wife, if she is working outside the home, will need to find a new job, as well. They need counseling. Additionally, they are in the most shame-filled, desperate moments of their lives. Never is a man more vulnerable, even suicidal, than when he is brought to public shame because of porn or sex addiction. This is not to excuse him—at all. But if the church is to be the body of Christ, she will not shoot her wounded. I suggest, whether your pastor—or any other staff member who falls—has been at your church for one year or twenty years, give him a minimum of six months' severance pay when he is dismissed. Make it a full year if at all possible. He needs time for personal recovery and restoration and to find his way forward with his calling and career. Forcing him to figure it all out with just one or two months of pay is brutal. In his darkest hour your pastor doesn't need justice—he needs mercy.

5. PLAN PROACTIVELY.

We have already said this. Have a plan in place before you need it. Assume that you will need to address this kind of issue at some point. If you prepare your buildings for the .7 percent who will need a wheelchair ramp, you should prepare your processes for the 50 percent of pastors who struggle with porn.

6. PROCEED COURAGEOUSLY.

Think big! What would it say to the world if you didn't fire your pastor? What if you put together a two-year plan by which he could return to his position, having concluded necessary counseling and treatment under careful supervision? Or if you feel he has disqualified himself from serving in this capacity and simply cannot remain in—or return to—his staff position, what if you brought him back to the church at a future point for the purpose of reconciliation and celebration? What if he completes successful therapy and finds lasting recovery, and you bring him in for a special occasion so he and his wife can share their story, make public amends, and receive the prayers and support of the church they served? What if the community saw you reconciling with your pastor in a way that was restorative and redemptive?

This takes courage. Any church can take their pastor's picture off the wall, remove him from the history books, and pretend he never existed. But is that what Jesus would do? At some point, one of your pastors or staff leaders will fall. Be ready. And when he or she does, think redemptively, respond biblically, react compassionately, provide financially, plan proactively, and proceed courageously!

A PLEA TO PASTORS

It has been my goal to offer a resource to the church. We seek to provide materials that will empower the body of Christ to talk about what nobody is talking about. It's not an easy subject to address in the halls of the local church, but we cannot afford to remain silent.

I want to close with a personal plea to pastors. For nearly 31 years I was one of you. I love everything about pastoring—except all the senseless meetings! I miss the preaching, administration, pastoral care, and vision casting. I miss the church staff meetings and retreats when we would plan the next year and dream of what could be for our discipleship ministry, student ministry, children's ministry, and worship.

What I don't miss is the pressure to perform, to always be "on." If you are a pastor, you get what I'm saying. It is that pressure (which non-ministers can't fully understand) that drives us to isolate, which creates a void, an emptiness. And that is where we become vulnerable to the trappings of sex and porn.

If that is you, reach out. That is what our ministry is all about. I wish I had had someone to turn to in my darkest hours and deepest valleys. But when you are "the man," who do you tell?

Earlier I quoted my friend, Michael Leahy, of *BraveHearts*, who says that only one in 10,000 finds recovery without the help of someone else. At *There's Still Hope*, we want to be that someone. I love to work with pastors, and Beth loves to work with their wives. (She's a lot better than I am!)

Pastor, if you are struggling with porn or sex addiction, with fantasy or lust, reach out— if not to us, to somebody. The enemy has you in his line of fire. He's coming for you because if he can bring you down, many others will likely fall as well.

Our website, TheresStillHope.org, offers a myriad of resources. I write a short devotional every day called *Recovery Minute*. I'd love to add you to my daily devotional list. We offer groups for addicts and their spouses. We offer one-day intensives and a 90-day customized recovery plan. But what really makes us different is our desire to help pastors. We are here for you. If you struggle with sex and porn issues, you are in the battle of your life, but you don't need to fight that battle alone.

ABOUT THE AUTHOR

Mark and Beth Denison are the founders and directors of *There's Still Hope*, a Christ-centered sexual addiction recovery ministry. Before launching TSH, Mark served as a senior pastor to three different churches in his home state of Texas. He also served as Board Chair at his alma mater, *Houston Baptist University*, and as a chaplain to the *Houston Rockets* for five seasons.

Mark has earned four degrees: Bachelor of Arts (*HBU*), Master of Divinity (*Southwestern Baptist Theological Seminary*), Master of Human Services, in Addiction Recovery (*Liberty University*), and Doctor of Ministry (*SWBTS*). Denison is an active member of the *American Association of Christian Counselors* (AACC).

Mark and Beth have been married since 1983, and they are the proud parents of one son. The

Denisons live in Bradenton, Florida, where they enjoy the Florida beaches and are active leaders in their local church. They enjoy travel, outdoor activities, and helping others find the recovery that they have discovered in their marriage and personal lives.

Before moving to Florida, Dr. Denison wrote Sunday school curriculum for Texas Baptists, The *Daily Walk* column for several newspapers, and had a daily radio broadcast, *One Minute Walk*.

Mark published his first book, *The Daily Walk*, in 2013. In addition to *Porn in the Pew*, Mark is the author of two more books on sexual addiction recovery: *90 Days to Recovery* and *365 Devotions for Personal Recovery*.

Suggested Resources

TWELVE-STEP PROGRAMS FOR SEX ADDICTION

- Sexaholics Anonymous (sa.org)
- Sex Addicts Anonymous (sexaa.org)
- Sex and Love Addicts Anonymous (slaafws.org)
- Sexual Recovery Anonymous (sexualrecovery. org)
- Castimonia (castimonia.org)

TWELVE-STEP PROGRAMS FOR SPOUSES

- S-ANON (sanon.org)
- Co-Dependents of Sex Addicts (cosa.recovery. org)

INTENSIVE OUTPATIENT SEX ADDICTION SERVICES

- Hope Quest (hopequest.org)
- Hope & Freedom Counseling Services (hope-andfreedom.com)
- Sexual Recovery Institute (sexualrecovery.com)

CHRIST-CENTERED WORKSHOPS

- Bethesda (bethesdaworkshops.org)
- Faithful & True (faithfulandtrue.com)
- Be Broken Ministries (bebroken.com)

About *There's Still Hope*

There's Still Hope is a comprehensive Christ-centered sexual addiction recovery ministry. With a focus on addicts, spouses, churches, and pastors, TSH has quickly become a leading resource for churches and schools. The ministry offers several unique recovery tools for those in need.

TSH is unlike other ministries for several reasons. Mark and Beth Denison work as a team, each with appropriate credentials. Mark has a Master's in Addiction Recovery, while Beth is certified as a Spouse Recovery Coach through the ministry of Dr. Doug Weiss.

There's Still Hope offers personal coaching for both addicts and their spouses. They also offer group work and one-day intensives, in addition to providing customized 90-day recovery plans. The ministry also presents programs for churches, high schools, and universities. Mark and Beth produce a daily "Recovery Minute" devotion and are regular contributors for *Covenant Eyes*.

To sign up for the daily devotional or to read more about *There's Still Hope*, visit the TSH website, at TheresStillHope.org.